Arnette
Heidkamp

A
HUMMINGBIRD
in
My
House

All that glitters is not gold. There are also diamonds, emeralds, rubies, and those living jewels, the hummingbirds.

A HUMMINGBIRD in My House

The Story of SQUEAK

Arnette Heidcamp

with photographs and drawings by the author

CROWN PUBLISHERS, INC., NEW YORK

Published by Crown Publishers, Inc., 201 East 50th Street, New York, New York 10022. Member of the Crown Publishing Group.

CROWN is a trademark of Crown Publishers, Inc.

Manufactured in Japan

Book design by Jennifer Harper

Library of Congress Cataloging-in-Publication Data

Heidcamp, Arnette
    A hummingbird in my house : the story of Squeak / by
Arnette Heidcamp—1st ed.
        p.   cm.
    1. Hummingbirds as pets.   2. Ruby-throated
hummingbird—New York (State)—Biography.
3. Heidcamp, Arnette.   I. Title.
SF473.H84H45   1990
636.6—dc20   90-2213
    ISBN 0-517-57729-1

10 9 8 7 6 5 4

A special thank you to my daughter for her help
with the photos of Squeak and me.

For Squeak, may he live a long and happy life,

and

for my friend and family who have lovingly
and quietly endured my passion for hummingbirds

Contents

A
HUMMINGBIRD
in
My
House

INTRODUCTION

I don't recall ever having seen a hummingbird while I was growing up except, perhaps, on television. They were from the tropics, or so I thought. It wasn't until years later when I moved to Upstate New York that I saw my first one. It was a thrill and I remember vividly my astonishment as I watched the unbelievably tiny and incredibly beautiful bird with the dazzling plumage flit boldly from flower to flower at no more than arm's length away. I told anyone who would listen what I had experienced; it was almost as if someone had bestowed some special privilege upon me and I was on cloud nine over my "discovery."

When I was young I was told that hummingbirds spend their entire lives in the air, that they never stop or rest. I remember wondering skeptically to myself, "How can that be? What about when they sleep? When they lay and sit on eggs?" Perhaps I even asked but never received an answer that made any impression. Anyway, I grew up halfheartedly believing it to be true. Only later, when I saw my first sitting hummingbird, I remember saying to myself, I knew it, I knew it and I also remember calling everyone around to come and look. The thrill of seeing a hummingbird has never left my heart.

Never did I dream that one day I'd hold two hummingbirds, one in each hand, or that one would sit on my finger and preen itself or feed from a flower that I held in my hand. Even in my wildest dreams I did not think I'd be sitting down to write a book about the one that stayed with me for the winter.

One cold, frostbitten day in late October 1988, long after all the other little hummingbirds had left for their sojourn in more tropical climes, I found a young male ruby-throated hummingbird (*Archilochus colubris*) in my garden. I did not know from where he had come, but I did know that, left on his own, he would die. Between high mortality during the first year, natural disaster, pollution, habitat destruction, and the general decline in hummers that has been reported over the last couple of years (responses given to questions fielded by *Bird Watchers* indicate that there is a real hummer decline), I feel that I did the right thing by taking this bird in. But only because I was able to offer suitable conditions, conducive to a healthy and nonfrustrating winter, did I keep him. Had I not thought that I would be able to provide exactly the conditions that he would need, I would have taken a different course of action.

People should lend a helping hand to nature when the need arises. That's what the people of Pt.

Barrow, Alaska, did for the trapped whales and that is what it is hoped that this effort has accomplished, saving one hummingbird from the sometimes cruel hands of nature. I have never been able to understand that let-nature-take-its-course attitude as witnessed on so many television documentaries. Instead of filming their demise under adverse conditions, people should help them out. Nature need not always run its course.

But, as much as I would like to have kept the hummingbird forever, I feel that I did the right thing by releasing it the following spring. My reward has been the experience of a lifetime.

Now I suppose I feel just the way I did when I saw my first hummingbird. I marvel no less now about these diminutive dynamos with their masterful aerial acrobatics and bold but captivating nature than I did then, and again I have to tell everyone what I have experienced, what special privilege has been bestowed upon me. I want to share this once-in-a-lifetime experience with everybody.

There have been other books about hummingbirds, very good ones. Paul A. Johnsgard's excellent, incomparable study of North American hummingbirds, *The Hummingbirds of North America* (Smithsonian Institution Press, 1983), will probably never be improved upon and it is without doubt the very best reference available. Alexander F. Skutch's *Life of the Hummingbird* (Crown, 1973) is informative and delightful, containing many interesting, personal anecdotes. The Tyrrells' *Hummingbirds—Their Life and Behavior* (Crown, 1985) is full of the most extraordinary and beautiful photographs available anywhere of the hummingbirds of the United States.

This book, however, is different. While I don't necessarily consider this a story, it's not technical in the true sense of the word, either. I prefer to consider this more of a documentary on paper, a factual but personal account of one individual hummingbird's unusual winter, from his arrival to the ultimate spring release of this lovable Lilliputian creature who, with his endearing ways, brought such a breath of springtime to every moment of my winter.

In some instances conclusions have been drawn based upon my personal observations not only of this bird but of the ruby-throats that have stopped in my garden over the years. If any of these observations yield an answer to but one unanswered question, I shall consider this a personal success.

1

How It All Began

October 20, 1988—that was to be the night to finish cutting back the fuchsias; killing frost was expected and temperatures would be dipping into the twenties. The fuchsias are grown and wintered over from year to year for the hummingbirds. I've always hated cutting them back and getting them ready for their dormant period because it means discarding perfectly beautiful flowers, but it had to be done and I had decided it was definitely time.

The prior week I had done some major pruning, getting ready for the move back indoors. *Salvia greggii*, even though it still had hundreds of blossoms, had to be cut back. Likewise the flowering maple (*Abutilon* hybrid), Island snapdragon (*Galvezia speciosa*), lantana, Chinese hibiscus, Chilean jasmine, and a *Mimulus puniceus* hybrid. Many were to be moved to a cool place where they would receive a winter dormancy period. Others, such as the orchids, would be spending the winter in the sunroom.

The majority of my plants are grown with hummingbirds in mind. From early May through late September, while the hummingbirds are here, my time is spent watching, photographing, and just enjoying them. The rest of the year is devoted to getting plants ready for the hummingbirds when they return the following spring—seeds are started for annuals, cuttings are taken from some plants, and tender perennials are cut back to begin anew. The last bird to have left this year did so on October 3 and as much as I wished it weren't, the season was definitely over.

The next morning I went outdoors, as I always do, for my early-morning ritual of putting seed in the bird feeders, changing the water in the birdbaths, and feeding a couple of stray cats. For some reason, my eyes drifted over to a patch of what had been *Salvia coccinea*. There were one or two remaining flowers behind leaves that had not been frosted the night before. I had to look twice—I thought I had seen a hummingbird. Then it appeared at what had been a patch of flowering tobacco. I couldn't believe my eyes, it was October 21 and all hummingbirds should have long been gone from this area. They generally leave

Upstate New York by late September or very early October at the latest, and the last date I've ever had one here has been October 10. I looked around and assessed the yard. The only flowers that were in a viable condition were the mums. I immediately dropped what I was doing, went into the house, prepared a nectar solution, and hung a feeder outside for the hummingbird. The bird flew into the lath house, a latticework structure used to house plants outdoors during the summer, and seemed to be looking around in the space where fuchsias had been the day before. My guess was that this was not its first visit to my yard but, since I had not seen it before, I figured that it had been here only for the one previous day.

I hung a four-flowers–type feeder filled with the nectar solution right behind the house where I was sure the bird would see it and placed a couple of flowering plants brought back outside near the feeder to entice the bird closer to it. I had no plan, I was merely concerned about the hummer having something to eat. The bird approached the feeder but obviously did not know what to do with it. It then visited the bouvardia plant and went back into the lath house looking, apparently, for the plants that had been there the day before. The poor thing must have been terribly hungry. What I noticed immediately about the bird was that it wasn't fat as they always are when they are ready to leave. This bird was not ready for migration and

*The new arrival.
With all the spotting
on its throat and chin,
I knew it was a male.*

the paltry amount of flowers that my garden had to offer was never going to be enough to sustain it while it fattened up and got ready to start its trip.

Certainly if the flowers in my garden were frosted, this bird would not be faring much better anyplace else. Even if a few hidden flowers here and there had made it through the frost, I wondered whether they would maintain their ability to produce nectar. Nectar production is richest under warm, sunny conditions and plant processes slow down under cool or cold conditions. I really didn't know what to do. The only thing I could think of was to try and get the bird into the house.

I've had hummingbirds in the house before, the first one during Hurricane Gloria in 1985. At that time I hung a feeder in the sunroom, opened the door, stuck a bare branch in the soil of a potted plant, and left it up to the bird to come in or not. One little female came in and spent about six hours, using the feeder and resting on the branch. As the hurricane subsided and the weather broke, other hummingbirds came around the house looking for the feeders. When she heard them outside, she would fly from window to window looking for the other birds. When one would come in, she'd chase it out. Eventually, she went outside. The next day I was afraid that she might fly into the glass on the door if she attempted to get back into the house, so I left the door open, but she never came back in again.

In 1987 we had a freak snowstorm on October 2 and while it wasn't as severe here along a strip of land on the western side of the Hudson River as it was farther away from the river, the weather was bad. While we did not have the broken branches and fallen trees that everyone else had, we did have wet snow in the morning. On that day I made a trail of flowering plants leading to the sunroom and got the last remaining hummingbird of the season to come into the house and then closed the door behind it. I kept her indoors for a couple of hours and released her when the sun came out and things warmed up and got back to normal.

I've also had young hummingbirds fly into the house, either chasing one another or alone, and land on the window screens. Some would fly in one window and out the other. Each one that has come in has reacted differently toward me. Two that came in together did absolutely nothing, they just sat in my hands; one chirped its little head off as I carried it outdoors to be released; and a third acted quite fussy, squirming all around and not wanting to be held at all.

Only 16 species of hummingbird, not counting accidentals, regularly reach the United States border. Of the 16 species that regularly visit the States, only one, the ruby-throated hummingbird (*Archilochus colubris*), visits the eastern part of the United States and Canada east of the middle of the Great Plains.

It's obvious that they gorge before they leave, a necessary part of migration. Although an occasional ruby-throat may overwinter as far north as Florida or Texas, their wintering grounds are from Mexico through Central America and they occasionally reach western Panama. They are reported to be rare winter residents in the Bahamas and Cuba and casual on some other West Indies islands. However, most cross the Gulf of Mexico, a nonstop, continuous flight of up to 500 miles, to reach their destinations. Fattening up beforehand adds the extra fuel necessary to make such a grueling trip. It has been estimated that most ruby-throats put on an additional 50 percent of their body weight in the last two to three weeks before migrating. They seem to stay until they fatten up to a certain point and then they leave. The ones who use the feeders invariably are the ones to leave first. The stragglers always seem to be the ones that don't know how to use the feeders. This little gem was obviously not fat enough to migrate and it didn't look as though he had even started to put on any extra weight at all. I was sure that he didn't know how to use feeders. By that late a time in October many should have been someplace between the mid- to southern-Atlantic states, with some having already arrived at their wintering grounds, but this one was still in Upstate New York. As a contrast to the way this bird looked, the little female who stayed in the house for the day in 1987 during the snowstorm was fat, with obvious extra weight in the breast and abdominal areas. While this little bird certainly was not scrawny, it was also obviously not ready to start a migration.

I've never had one stay overnight, however, so I was concerned. If I were able to get the bird into the house, what then? How long could I keep it? If I took a couple of hours away from it, might that work more to its detriment than its good? I wanted it to eat. I wanted to teach it how to use the feeder. I decided I would try to get it inside.

Again, I placed a trail of flowers leading from the porch to the back door and inside the sunroom the way I did with that little female the year before. I stood at the door and when the hummingbird came in, I closed the door behind it. I then set up some branches on which the bird could sit and tried to teach it how to use a feeder. This time I used a small Perky bottle, a glass gravity-type feeder with a feeding tube and bee guard, but I did not use the bee guard that came with it. Instead, I took one of the red stoppers from another feeder, placed it on the tip of the feeding tube, and held that feeder in my hand among the bouvardia flowers. The bird went from flower to flower at the bouvardia and it also visited the feeder. Needless to say, the nectar in the feeder was sweet and abundant. The bird liked it and came back repeatedly. I then attached the feeder to a wire and the hummer proceeded to use the feeder regularly for the rest of the day.

Each year when the fall migration began I would dream of how wonderful it would be if I were to have a hummingbird spend the winter in my sunroom so I might appreciate it for all twelve months of the year instead of just five. This could be a dream-come-true and, while it was what I had always dreamed of, depriving the bird of its freedom wasn't what I really wanted. I knew the bird needed more than just nectar; it also needed protein. Hummingbirds will eat 400 to 500 insects every day. Where would I get the protein? What might I add to the diet to make it complete? I certainly did not want to hurt the bird by failing to provide what it needed and I did not want to interfere with nature by preventing the bird from following its instincts; but, I also did not want the bird to die. To help make my decision, I made a few telephone calls.

I placed my first call to a local bird veterinarian and told him that I had a hummingbird in the house, that I was concerned about it being here so late in the season, and asked him about a protein supplement. He told me that, unfortunately, he had not had any experience with hummingbirds.

I then called the Cornell Lab at Ithaca and spoke with a gentleman who had a couple of suggestions for me. First, he told me, the mortality rate for hummingbirds in their first year is 60 to 80 percent and that this bird "probably was not going to make it." He suggested that I either keep the bird all winter, if I could provide suitable conditions for it, keep the bird three or four days until it fattened up and release it on a nice day, or find someone who was going south and who would be willing to take the bird along and release it somewhere between the mid-Atlantic states and Florida. Keeping it for three or four days entered my mind. I knew that I would be able to provide enough nectar for it and thought that, hopefully, it would fatten up and be in better condition to leave in a day or two. However, three or four days later would be three or four days later, and if nothing was available outside for it to eat today, there would not be anything available tomorrow either. Sending it down with someone to the mid-Atlantic states was not a feasible idea, all things considered, and I ruled that out. The only suggestion left for me was to keep the bird; I knew I certainly could provide it with suitable conditions. After all, the sunroom is 12 by 15 feet, on a separate heat zone, with three sides of glass and filled to the brim with flowering plants. But still, there was the problem of supplying protein to the bird. Without protein in its diet, the bird would die. It couldn't live on nectar alone. I'd read of someone who cared for orphaned ruby-throats by adding a drop of cow's blood to nectar for protein, but I could not imagine that such a measure would produce long-term balanced, satisfactory, or beneficial results. And, while it might be a possible emergency measure, it is doubtful that it would be suitable for long-term nourishment.

My next call was to the San Diego Zoo, which I knew to have a hummingbird aviary. The person with whom I spoke at San Diego thought it was a wonderful idea that I keep the bird. She told me that the folks there use Nektar-Plus as a complete diet for hummingbirds but thought that I might have difficulty obtaining it since it is not generally available to the public. In the meantime, she suggested that I get some fruit flies and release them in the room with the hummingbird for it to eat, which I did; but having a constant supply of several hundred on hand at all times was going to be a real problem and I was concerned. I wanted to help the bird and I wanted to give it every chance to live. I was afraid that it would die if it didn't stay here but certainly the last thing I wanted to do was contribute to its dying anyway.

If I were going to keep this bird, I would have to make some changes not only in my routine, but in the conditions that I kept for the plants as well. In other years I ran a ceiling fan in the sunroom for circulation around the plants and general heat conservation. That would be out of the question this year. I made sure that it was shut off not only at the wall switch outside the sunroom but in the sunroom at the fan itself. Insecticides would also be out. I never use any insecticides outdoors, but I had always moved plants to the garage and sprayed them each fall before bringing them inside.

If I were to keep the bird, I would have also have to be concerned about how to keep it from getting fat. After all, this is the time of year when its natural inclination is to fatten up for its trip south and it may only be retarded, not lacking, in this respect. I don't know what causes the fattening-up process. I don't know if it has to do with day length, temperature, or insect availability. Or it may be a specific hormone produced by certain birds or animals that causes them to overeat—perhaps a growth hormone. Even if that were so, some external or internal monitor would have to trigger production of that hormone. Perhaps it's all in the DNA. Of course, adult males leave by the end of August and the insects are certainly available at that time of year. Temperature varies from year to year but they do generally leave about the same time each year. The only consistency I could think of was day length. Perhaps that does have something to do with it. To combat that, in case that was the answer, I would be leaving lights on in excess of twelve hours per day in the sunroom. I know what difference this makes when growing daylight-sensitive plants, and this could be the key to keeping the bird from preparing for its migration.

My next step was to call the local pet store. Liz, the owner, very kindly contacted the manufacturer of Nektar-Plus and arranged to have some shipped UPS Next Day Air and delivered the very next day to me.

In the meantime, I had flowers for the bird, the nectar solution in the hanging feeders, and I caught some spiders to give him. I hunted through all my plants and found all the small spiders I could and held them in front of the bird by the web. With each spider held up, the bird gobbled it down and, while its mouth was opened, appeared to be smiling.

I thought over and over again that perhaps I should reconsider finding someone to take the bird south to release it there but, as the days went on, I knew that wouldn't be happening. The bird certainly seemed to be content and I was absolutely delighted. I think that deep down I knew right from the start that it would be staying until the spring.

I called the bird Squeak because of its constant squeaky chirping. With all the spotting on its throat and chin, I knew it was a male and, after a couple of days, I saw his first iridescent red spot. He had only been in my sunroom a couple of days, but already he had captured my heart and I was anticipating watching the change from young male hummer to a beautiful resplendent adult. I would do everything possible to keep him happy and healthy and I planned to release him in the spring. Of course, this too might turn out to be a problem: He might not want to leave. I hoped, of course, that he would because I wanted him to live a normal hummingbird life, but I'd probably enjoy it if he didn't. I remember when we, my two sisters and I, were young, we always found young "injured" birds to bring home to our parents. Each bird that was brought home was taken care of, primarily by my mother, and released when it was ready. But I do remember different birds, robins mostly, who had been released and would fly out one window and fly right back in another. They didn't want to leave. One robin that had been taken care of by my mother would land on her shoulder whenever she was in the yard. One day it disappeared and, presumably, migrated with the other robins. The following spring that same bird came back and landed on her shoulder again—a year later! So it's very possible that this humming-bird might find the safety here more appealing and not want to leave the way many other wild and caged birds do. I thought that I would cross that bridge when I came to it.

2

Daily Activities And Habits

The Morning

Each morning was basically the same, with variations on the theme, and although the rituals changed from time to time, he was such a little creature of habit. When the lights went on at the beginning of the day, he would waken and the first thing he would do was swallow, probably emptying his crop. His tongue would then dart in and out, he would flap his tail, shake out his wings, and then go into his stretching routine. He stretched both wings backward and then, unilaterally, first one side, then the other. The wings were stretched straight down along each side; then both wings were stretched backward again while he simultaneously fanned his tail. He took a couple of minutes each morning to bring his body temperature back up to its normal 102 to 108 degrees F.

Immediately thereafter he would eat. He would first visit the feeder at the south end of the room

At the beginning of the day the wings were stretched straight down along each side.

During his morning ritual Squeak stretched both wings backward while he simultaneously fanned his tail.

Eventually his choice sitting spot of the morning became a certain branch at the south end of the room.

and then sit for a few minutes on a certain branch near the window scratching his head and chin before returning to the feeder.

During this morning ritual he would then make visits to the various flower spikes for accumulated nectar, returning to the feeder and, finally, to his choice sitting spot of the time. The sitting spot changed from time to time. During October and most of November, it was a certain phalaenopsis spike only inches beneath the fluorescents. Later the choice spot became the rounded bottom of a wire designed to clamp to the edge of a flowerpot, but in this case inverted and used as a stake, again only inches below the fluorescents. Still later the choice morning spot became a two-inch piece of metal bar at the end of a tray frame. Eventually

21

and finally it became a certain branch at the south end of the room.

By the time the first day of spring arrived, it was quite light outside when the lights went on at 6:00 A.M. Robins and cardinals could be heard by 5:45 A.M. On the first day of spring, March 20, Squeak began to stir before the lights went on. By March 23, he was waking and starting his routine before the lights, but Daylight Savings begins in early April and so none of this continued for very long. Daylight Savings brings lighter evenings and, although Squeak was much more active in general than he had been all winter, he seemed to be more positively affected by the extra natural light at the end of his day than at the beginning. Continued lengthening days brought increased activity and before the end of April he was again stirring and feeding before the lights went on. By the time the first week in May was over, Squeak was starting to rouse at 5:30 A.M.

Squeak also enjoyed flying around the room. This is something that was routinely done each morning and I believe it was done purely for exercise. Not all the time, but more often than not he would fly in a counterclockwise direction. I wondered if the direction of his path would reverse itself in the spring, but it didn't. Squeak spent an average of ten minutes each morning exercising this way.

The Bath

It was then time to bathe. Hummingbirds love to bathe and they do so in a number of ingenious ways and frequently. They shower in the rain or the spray from under a waterfall, bathe in pools of water on rocks or leaves, fly into wet leaves and rub on wet moss.

I bought a small plastic birdbath for Squeak right away. It is essential for a bird to keep its feathers clean and I had hoped that he would learn to use it. Instead, by his third day here, I realized he had different plans.

On most mornings I mist the plants in the sunroom, wetting the roots and leaves from a spray bottle for a little extra humidity. On the third morning, no sooner had I finished than Squeak flew over and began to slide around on the leaf of the phalaenopsis plant that I had been misting. He was obviously trying to get all of his underparts wet, his breast, under his wings, and his chin. He certainly seemed to be enjoying himself. All the

23

Waiting for his bath, Squeak watches while I wet the cattleya leaf.

Squeak slides around on the cattleya leaf to get his underparts wet.

Notice how wet Squeak has become.

Even the chin is cleaned; note the closed eyes.

while he was bathing, sliding around and sliding down the phalaenopsis leaf and wetting his throat, breast, and underwings, he was chirping. It was obvious that what he was doing was very, very pleasurable. After bathing for a few minutes, he would fly around the room, undoubtedly to dry his feathers. The wet wing and tail feathers produce a very sharp sound when wet. With the air passing through the feathers the way it does, the sound is like a deck of cards being shuffled. He would then return to the feeder for a drink and go back to the phalaenopsis spike, sit and wait for me to mist some more so he might bathe all over again. After hummingbirds bathe, they like to preen. Squeak really enjoyed bathing on that phalaenopsis leaf and he wanted to do it every morning.

One Saturday in early November, I bought a bromeliad on a driftwood arrangement consisting of two small tillandsias on the wood and, at the bottom, a neoreglia that holds plenty of water in its cup. I thought Squeak might use this as a place to bathe, but he didn't show any interest in it at first. He had developed the habit of using that phalaenopsis leaf and returned to it over and over again even though there were other leaves in the sunroom that were wetter than that plant's leaf.

I know that hummingbirds enjoy bathing and I've watched them in the garden approaching the spray from a hose that was deliberately left on just for that purpose. I've read about birds flying through the water over and over again, using the spray as a slide, but they haven't done it here. Anna's hummingbird apparently has done that. I don't know whether the ruby-throat will or not, but they will approach the water out of curiosity.

There have been times when I've watched one hummingbird or another during a rain. The bird would sit out on the clothesline with its head facing upward, arch its back and spread its wing and tail feathers, trying to get its entire back wet. After two or three minutes it would shake off all the water, only to start the same routine all over again.

One morning in mid-November Squeak showed some interest in the actual spraying of "his" phalaenopsis and the other plants by approaching the spray of water and hovering in front of it to check it out. When he returned to his branch I let the spray flow in his direction. Immediately, even before the water touched him, he fanned his tail in anticipation. I directed it over him lightly so several drops fell on his back. He loved it, acting the same way the others have acted while sitting on the clothesline in the rain. Afterward he rubbed his chin over the branch where he had been perching, making sure that every available drop touched him. The shower would last for several minutes. Squeak let me know when he'd had enough by backing away from the spray and flying to a branch on the other side of the room where he would sit and

Squeak loved to bathe; all the while he bathed he would chirp.

Squeak receiving his daily shower.

Finally in mid-November Squeak bathed on the bromeliad leaves.

The wings are cleaned by the bill.

preen for at least fifteen minutes. He would dry off by shaking the water out of his wings and tail. Then he would run his beak over the wing feathers on one side, shake out the flight feathers again, run his beak over the feathers on the opposite side, and shake out again. This action was repeated over and over again until he appeared to be satisfied that he was dry enough. This became a daily morning ritual. Within a week he knew so well what the spray bottle meant that he would fly to the branch and chirp repeatedly in anticipation while going through all the motions of his shower. All this before feeling even one drop.

On some mornings, however, he had to make a game of it first. He would go through all the motions waiting for the shower. Then, the minute I began spraying him, he would take off, straight at my face, detour around my head at the very last instant, fly to the other side of the room, and then return to the branch to do it all again. This behavior would go on for several moments. Finally, after five or six tries to get started, Squeak would settle down for the shower.

In mid-November he bathed on the bromeliad leaves. First he pecked at the drops of water on the leaves and then he bathed. The edges of the leaves of neoreglia are wavy and slightly rough or spiny. He looked twice at the leaves, being more used to the hard, smooth, and somewhat waxy leaves of the phalaenopsis. He did not, however, place his body in the cup and the bromeliad was always a second-choice bath.

My main reason for getting that bromeliad arrangement for Squeak was so that a source of water would be available to him for the whole day. Even though I wet down all the various leaves in the room, they dried off rather quickly and I wasn't always available to do this repeatedly during the day. I had hoped that he would make use of the bromeliad's cup of water during the day just as I had hoped he would do when I offered the plastic birdbath, but he hadn't. As long as there were wet leaves around, that's what he used, except, of course, for his shower. It didn't matter whether the leaves were on fuchsia plants, the flowering maple, or the gardenia, he would fly into them and rub against the leaves to get his body wet.

Eventually I stopped using the phalaenopsis leaf and switched him over to one on a cattleya plant. The benefits of using the cattleya leaf were twofold. First, its leaf is more horizontal and waxy than the phalaenopsis leaf and would therefore, hold the water longer and give him a better surface on which to bathe. Also, the worry of water sitting in the crown of the phalaenopsis was eliminated with the use of the cattleya. He accepted the switch happily. But I still hadn't found an answer to my problem of how to keep bathing water available for the whole day, and in a container that he would accept.

Feathers are fastidiously separated and the bill is drawn over them.

Wherever they can be reached, feathers are done one at a time.

Hummingbirds must resort to scratching to clean the head, neck, and throat areas.

The beak is frequently cleaned with the feet.

Then, knowing that many hummingbirds will bathe in the spray from waterfalls, I decided to make one for Squeak. I searched far and wide looking for the component parts that I would need for its construction. Finally I found a sizable piece of lava rock with which to work and was able to locate a submersible, recirculating pump for the water. What I wanted was to have the water flow from the top of the rock to two or three small, shallow pools at different levels below it. In addition, I wanted to have three or four pockets in other parts of the lava rock in which I might place small flowering plants. I began work on the waterfall early in January, chiseling out the pools, crevices, and pockets with a small chisel and hammer and, for every four or five times that I hit the chisel with the hammer, I hit my hand once. It was hard, time-consuming work, but eventually it was completed. The rock was decorated with a couple of angraecum orchids and a bromeliad in its pockets; the water was turned on, and it worked beautifully. I was happy to know that a source of water would now be available for Squeak at all times. He investigated it immediately, as he did with everything, but he didn't show any interest in using it for bathing. I hoped that eventually, as with the bromeliad, that would change, but it didn't. Perhaps if the daily bath and shower weren't provided for him, he might have taken more interest in the waterfall as a possible bathing or shower area.

Once I hooked it up he stayed near it most of the day. It became his favorite hunting area, as he could always find an insect or two there and perhaps he liked the sound of trickling water. Once the waterfall was hooked up, he seldom sat under the fluorescents except, that is, for his bath and shower. The one thing that remained most constant during his entire stay was his love of the bath and shower.

Preening

Squeak spent more of his time perching than anything else. Much of that perching time was spent preening and generally fussing over himself. Hummingbirds give their feathers a great deal of care. During preening a hummingbird touches its bill to the uropygial, or preening gland, a skin gland located near the base of its tail, to collect oil for cleaning and waterproofing its wings, tail feath-

35

After each feeding Squeak would clean his beak on a twig.

At times Squeak would sunbathe, fluffing up and exposing himself to the sun.

36

Occasionally a loose
feather would stick
to Squeak's tongue.

Using his foot to
remove the feather from
his tongue.

ers, back, and abdomen, and for lubricating its bill and legs. The wings, tail, back, and abdomen are cleaned by the bill. Feathers are fastidiously separated and the bill is drawn over them. The tail is lifted and arched laterally toward the beak while the tail feathers are spread apart with the beak pulling through each tail feather. The head is also turned toward the back, enabling the bird to run its beak across the upper tail coverts. Wherever they can be reached, feathers are done one at a time, a long and painstaking process.

However, since hummingbirds cannot reach all of their feathers and do not engage in mutual preening, they must resort to scratching to clean the head, neck, and throat areas. The head is bent to place its feathers, as well as the feathers of the neck and throat, in a position to be reached by the claws. Hummingbirds scratch frequently, often without displaying any other preening behavior.

The feet and legs are cleaned with the bill by a nibbling action and the beak itself is cleaned either on a twig or branch or with the feet. After each feeding, Squeak would clean his beak on a twig.

One of the funniest things that Squeak would do was scratch while he was flying or, more correctly, scratching in midair. Usually he scratched his head, but at times it appeared that he may also have been pecking at a foot. He was probably cleaning it; I noticed that he would engage in that behavior most often after a bath or shower than at any other time. At times, however, he would raise his foot while hovering, obviously to clean his beak. While he was so occupied, this little acrobat would descend in a spiral motion toward the floor, just about managing to stay up.

Squeak spent a great deal of time preening. At times he would "sunbathe," fluffing up and exposing himself to the sun, and sitting at the window in that same position for quite a while. Afterward he would scratch the warmed areas.

Several times while Squeak was vigorously scratching himself, he fell from his branch. Each time he would immediately right himself in midair, go back to where he had been sitting, and start scratching all over again. Such an acrobat, such perfect control, no struggling, so matter-of-factly and naturally, he'd hardly miss a beat.

Squeak spent a tremendous amount of time scratching and preening during his molt—much more than usual, although that hardly seems possible. Preening, scratching, and shaking out helped him to get rid of loose feathers and pinfeather sheaths. Occasionally a loose feather would stick to his tongue. He would try two or three times to rid himself of it by drawing his tongue in and pushing it back out again, but invariably this was best accomplished when he adeptly used his foot as though it were a hand and just pulled the feather from the tongue.

Shaking out helped Squeak get rid of loose feathers and pinfeather sheaths.

Fuchsias are almost magnetic to hummingbirds.

Flowers and Food

Metabolism is the process by which food is turned into energy. Because of their size and lifestyle, hummingbirds have a very high rate of metabolism, producing a tremendous amount of needed energy. They have the greatest energy output, relatively, of any warm-blooded animal. Accordingly, they require great quantities of food.

The hummingbird's primary source of nourishment is nectar, a renewable, easily digested and quickly converted source of energy. Nectar is composed of various sugars. Of all the sugars, sucrose is the one that is preferred.

Through simultaneous evolution, hummingbirds have become most suited to extract nectar from flowers and, at the same time, many flowers have evolved to become particularly suited for pollination by hummingbirds. Hummers can frequently be seen with a dusting of pollen on their foreheads, crowns, or beaks. These "hummingbird flowers" usually have an abundant store of nectar, containing approximately 25 percent sugar; are more or less tubular in shape and somewhat open on the inflorescences; have no fragrance, since odorless flowers are unattractive to insects; pollen is quite often located outside of the flower and flowers very often have elongated anthers and no "landing platform," making the nectar less accessible to insects. Hummingbird-adapted flowers are attractive in color. Attractive means noticeable. Red flowers are the flowers of choice because they are most noticeable. However, in the shade many hummingbird flowers are of an orange color, which is more noticeable under such conditions. Hummingbird flowers are attractive primarily to hummingbirds.

Certain hummingbirds prefer certain flowers, the primary reason why so many different species can coexist in the tropics. By and large, small hummingbirds prefer small flowers and large hummingbirds prefer large flowers. The nectary in a large flower may be out of reach for a small hummingbird and there is not usually enough nectar in a small flower to make it worthwhile for a large hummingbird to expend the energy necessary to visit it. Hummingbirds with odd-shaped bills are adapted to odd-shaped flowers. The swordbill with daturas and the white-tipped sicklebill with heliconia are two good examples that may be cited.

In the United States there are many humming-bird-adapted flowers. There is even a species of cactus, the hedgehog, that is pollinated exclusively by a hummingbird. Some plants that are noted as being particularly suited to pollination by the ruby-throated hummingbird are cardinal flower (*Lobelia cardinalis*), jewelweed or touch-me-not (*Impatiens capensis*), and bee balm (*Monarda didyma*). I've grown many different flowers in my garden for humming-birds, including all those mentioned above, but from my own experience, the two favorites are tropical salvia (*Salvia coccinea*) and the red varieties of bee balm.

Knowing which flowers yield the richest stores of nectar is not something hummingbirds know from birth. They must learn which of the flowers contain nectar and they learn by trial and error. Tremendous curiosity will drive nestlings to try everything, even roses. Coupled with that curios-ity is an excellent memory. They remember, even a year later, where the "good stuff" was. One early May morning a couple of years ago I was able to witness the return of one of our regular males. He arrived in the yard, stopped momentarily on the clothesline, and then immediately turned left and went under the pine tree to where his favorite feeder had been the year before. Of course it was there again. The point is, not only was the bird

Squeak visits the flowering maple.

*Squeak is very fond of
the nectar that forms
on parts of certain
orchid plants.*

All of a sudden Squeak loved the Aerangis hybrid.

Squeak loved bromeliads.

45

driven to the same breeding grounds as the year before, but after an absence of eight months, he remembered where to find a favorite source of food. Even after seeing such displays of memory over and over again, it still amazes me.

To what degree Squeak's association with our flowers parallels that which would occur in the wild is unknown, at least to me. Take fuchsias for instance. Flowers of the fuchsia plants are notorious hummingbird favorites. Indeed, one of the quickest ways to attract hummers to your feeders is to place the feeder in close proximity to fuchsia plants. Fuchsias are almost magnetic to hummingbirds. In the fall my fuchsias are cut back, usually in two or three steps, and then stored in a cool place until late December when they are taken out and put under the lights in the basement to start their new growth cycle. It was after the first pruning session that Squeak made his appearance in our yard and after having been cut back, flowers on the fuchsias were sparse. *Fuchsia triphylla* hybrids, such as Gartenmeister Bonstedt, are particularly attractive to hummers and will flower all winter long if given cool evenings, 60 degrees F., or below. That was one plant that was not affected by the cutting back and was made immediately available to Squeak. His interest in that plant was, surprisingly, lacking. Because of Squeak's arrival, the others were immediately put under the basement lights and began to grow again, with new flower buds visible shortly thereafter. As, one by one, they began to flower, they were moved into the sunroom. Squeak visited them but never showed the same avid interest in these flowers that had always been shown by other hummers. Why? What would make a favorite flower of the summer now become second choice—even when the total number of choices had narrowed? Perhaps fuchsias are reserved for the dominant hummingbirds on the wintering grounds. Maybe they are not producing the nectar indoors that they do outside. Is it an instinctive action to shy away from flowers that under normal and ordinary conditions would be off limits?

Sleeping hibiscus (*Malvaviscus arboreus*), so called because the flowers never fully open, is another example. Apparently *Malvaviscus arboreus* is considered the choice tubular flower in its habitat. Nectar from it is dominated by the superior resident hummers, while nectar from the less productive cup-shaped flowers is left for the subordinates who forage at such flowers. I grow *Malvaviscus arboreus*, but Squeak never seemed to show any interest in this supposedly choice flower. Although he did approach its flowers on one or two occasions, it almost seemed that he avoided the plant. Maybe it is instinctively forbidden because of the subordinate status that he would have had on his wintering grounds. There are so many questions! He did not, however, avoid the little cup-shaped flowers of

He especially loved tillandsias; here he visits T. geminiflora.

Squeak visits T. juncea.

Squeak used his beak to raise tubular, hanging flowers to a horizontal position.

Insects are captured in a variety of ways; here Squeak captures a whitefly.

flowering maple. It has been my observation that this is a plant ordinarily left for the subordinates. Here, in our garden, the dominant hummers have always claimed the fuchsias while the subordinates would sneak in while the "yard boss" wasn't looking to visit abutilon and impatiens plants, both of which have always been ignored by the dominant hummers. I suppose that I should mention here that Squeak also visited the large impatiens plant regularly. I wanted to know what his attitude was going to be toward these very same flowers when and if he became an aggressive, territorial, and, hopefully, dominant adult ruby-throated hummingbird.

Beside flowers, there are other sources of nectar available to hummingbirds, especially ruby-throats. They are notorious for visiting sapsucker holes—more frequently than any other birds, including the sapsucker woodpeckers who drilled them. In a study by Foster and Tate, it was noted that of the four hummingbird species to visit sapsucker feeding trees (ruby-throat, Anna's, broad-tailed and rufous), the ruby-throat was not only observed most frequently but was the only one to systematically collect insects in the vicinity. This sap may even offer sustenance to birds returning early in spring while flowering is still sparce.

Few orchids contain any nectar and those that do are not readily accessible to hummingbirds. Many are pollinated through mimicry, the ability of the flower to resemble and attract its pollinator.

There are a few New World orchids, however, that do depend upon hummingbirds for pollination: *Comparetta falcata*, *Laelia milleri*, and *Elleanthus capitatus*. Nevertheless, many orchids, such as the Cattleya alliance orchids, produce a thick and sticky nectar-like substance along the inflorescence, sometimes on the pseudobulb and on the flower stems at the base of the petals. Squeak is very fond of this nectar, as are, I'm sure, other hummingbirds, and he visits the plants several times each day looking for the accumulation. This "honey" is more copious before flowering begins and some plants just drip with it. I grow many orchids and except for the honey that is produced, they are, for the most part, useless as a food source for Squeak. Orchids in the Angraecum family are an exception. Angraecum orchids and their allies, Aerangis and Aeranthes, are Old World orchids coming from Africa, Madagascar, the Comoros and some other Indian Ocean islands. They are almost always white, some are highly fragrant, especially at night, and most have a spur, which can be extremely long, containing nectar. They are usually pollinated by moths. One in particular, a little aerangis hybrid, has white flowers about one and one-half inches across with the usual long spur and an orange column. I showed them to Squeak in an attempt to pique his interest, but I couldn't get him to pay any attention to those flowers at all—at first. Then one day he discovered the aerangis and all of a

Squeak had no problem spotting insects; here he prepares to go after one.

A specially designed feeder was chosen for Squeak.

Drawing from the reserve in his crop

Visiting Abutilon megapotamicum.

sudden he loved them. I was able to see him slide his tongue, which would be greatly extended beyond the tip of his bill, under the column and into the spur. Considering the amount of time spent on these flowers in comparison to others, it would be my guess that this plant produces copious amounts of nectar.

Another orchid that Squeak spent much time with was *Phragmipedium schlimii*, a South American terrestrial lady slipper with an exquisite roselike fragrance. Instead of attempting to get at the nectar through the slipper part, the way an insect would do, Squeak ingeniously found a way to stick his beak in through the back of the flower, behind the slipper.

Whenever possible, Squeak would perch while eating. At times he perched on one of his branches; at other times a leaf stem came in handy as a place to sit; he was frequently found perching on the edge of one flowerpot or another, stretching his neck to reach a desired flower; and, when flowers were large enough, he would perch on the petals. Squeak loved hibiscus flowers. While visiting them he would very often hold on to the edge of the flower with his claws to keep his balance while lowering his head deep within the blossom. I've frequently seen other hummingbirds do the same thing with the hibiscus relative, rose of sharon. Squeak was so fond of hibiscus that he wouldn't even wait for them to unfurl. Instead he pierced numerous holes in the petals with his beak, trying to get nectar before the flowers were ready to open.

In their native habitats, tillandsias, members of the Bromeliad family, are pollinated primarily by hummingbirds. While Squeak never visited the flowers of the neoreglia plant, he loved bromeliads, and especially tillandsias, better than everything else.

I noticed on several occasions that Squeak would use his beak to raise tubular, hanging flowers to a horizontal position. Perhaps in that way nectar that had accumulated in a particular flower would be concentrated on just one side of the tube and, therefore, more conveniently available.

To survive, hummingbirds also require a diet adequate in protein, carbohydrates, fats, vitamins, and minerals. That need is supplied by minute insects and small spiders, which are slower to digest than the sugars are. Insects and spiders are captured in a variety of ways. Some are probably occasionally taken from within the flowers incidental to drinking, but basically they are either plucked off branches, twigs, leaves, trees, flowers, and walls, or captured in flight. Many times I have watched the nightly occurrence of a hummingbird sitting on the clothesline waiting for a swarm of small insects, probably gnats, to get closer. When the swarm is near, the hummingbird dives in and flits around taking one insect after another. I've noticed

Squeak visited most available flowers; here he visits snapdragons.

this behavior more on rainy days than on sunny ones and more in the evenings than during other times of the day. It could be that more insects are eaten at that time because more are available. It might also be that nectar production in flowers is richer during the sunny weather. It is reported that more nectar is secreted on sunny days, increasing with higher, dry temperatures and decreasing with humidity or moisture. When flowers are scarce, and most likely if nectar production is down, hummingbirds depend very heavily upon insects to supplement their diet. Some insects are even stolen from spiders' webs. As a matter of fact, if the spider is small enough, it would be eaten as well.

Squeak had no problem seeing an insect from

Visiting kalanchoe.

across the room and, since I didn't use any insecticide this year, there was always an abundant supply available for him. He'd pluck them from the windows, walls, and leaves. Very often he'd sit on a branch just waiting for one to go by and grab it. When Squeak noticed an insect that he wanted, he would open his mouth wide, dip below the insect and come up, closing his beak on it and swallow. Afterward, he'd sometimes glide across the room with his mouth opened in a vertical position, almost as if to help the bug go down. I have also watched him do this after taking nectar from one or the other of the feeders. He may have been getting some sediment from the solution and was trying to get it down.

Insects form a very important part of the hummingbird's diet. For many years it was presumed that hummingbirds existed only on sugars and the estimates of their consumption of sugars in ratio to body size were grossly exaggerated. When hummingbirds kept in aviaries could not be kept alive on diets consisting only of sugar, people began to believe that it was actually the insects in the flowers to which the hummingbirds were attracted. It was soon discovered, however, that hummingbirds could no more exist on an all-protein diet than they could on an all-sugar diet. Studies conducted by Walter Scheithauer concluded that a hummingbird's diet must consist of a balance between nectar and insects and revealed much about hummingbirds' digestion in general.

Right from the start, offering a balanced diet to Squeak was my foremost concern. With this balance in mind, the diet that was suggested to and chosen by me was Nektar-Plus, made by the Nekton company. Nektar-Plus is a complete diet made specifically for hummingbirds, sunbirds, honeycreepers, and bananaquits, and containing a balanced selection of carbohydrates, protein, fat, vitamins, minerals and trace elements, all chosen to complement one another. In short, a complete and balanced diet. The protein in Nektar-Plus comes from eighteen different, pure amino acids duplicating that which has been found in hummingbirds' stomachs. Carbohydrates are in the form of glucose, fructose, and sucrose, corresponding to natural flower nectars. Nektar-Plus comes in a powdered form but is easily mixed with water. It truly took only seconds each day to prepare Squeak's food.

The only drawback to feeding Nektar-Plus is its tendency, like that of any other protein solution, to spoil over the course of a day. However, when used in conjunction with Nekton's special disinfectant, it is possible to keep the Nektar-Plus solution longer, thereby making it unnecessary to mix the formula more than once each day. The specially designed brown Plexiglas feeders offered by the Nekton people were chosen for their ability to filter light rays, thus preventing the decay of important vitamins, and for the sloping bottom of the tube, which would give Squeak access to any components not completely water-soluble. Two sets of two feeders each were used altogether; two tubes were used in the sunroom each day while the other two were soaking in the disinfectant all day long, removed to air-dry overnight and replaced daily just before Squeak wakened. No introduction to this feed was necessary; Squeak accepted and, undoubtedly, liked it from the time that he first tried it.

Two feeders were kept going at all times in case, by slim chance, one leaked or emptied during the day. One was kept on the east side of the room, the other on the south. Generally, neither location seemed to be preferred over the other.

The return of spring brought many new flowers for Squeak to try; here he visits Korean rhododendron.

However, Squeak, apparently preferring either light or warmth, would visit the feeder on the south side of the room on sunny days; on cloudy days and especially evenings, the feeder on the east side of the room and near the fluorescents was preferred. Use of the feeders was direct and without fanfare except at night—and only with the east feeder. During the last hour or so before Squeak went to sleep and every time he visited that feeder, he would take a sip and then drop down and to the right of the feeder about three to four feet. This strange action occurred after each sip. I have never been able to figure out why. Squeak visited most available flowers and caught lots of insects and spiders, but Nektar-Plus remained his staple.

Branches of flowering apricot were brought in for Squeak.

I enjoyed watching Squeak eat and I watched him at every available opportunity. When a hummingbird eats, its tongue flicks rapidly in and out of its bill. When the tongue is pushed out of the tightly closed bill, nectar from the flower which the bird is visiting is drawn into the grooves of the tongue by capillary action. The tongue is then drawn back into the slightly opened bill. Then, when the bird repeats the action of pushing its tongue out of the tightly closed bill, the collected nectar is forced into the oral cavity. This cycle takes less than one-tenth of a second. Once I learned the mechanics, I tried to glimpse one of the secrets from his tiny world—I wanted to see it for myself.

Hummingbirds feed frequently. An average of once every 10 to 15 minutes is usually given. What food is not immediately used is stored in the crop for later consumption. Two or three times between each visit to the feeder, Squeak would draw from the reserve in his crop. Swallowing action could be noted by the movement in his gorget area. After each three or four swallows, he would then open his mouth to quite a wide position. After the last series of swallows and gulp, his tongue would dart in and out, an action associated with the act of feeding, and he would then visit the feeder. He probably visited the feeder whenever he found his crop empty. However, this action took place primarily during periods of lessened activity, such as very late afternoons and evenings before going to sleep. He also swallowed in that manner frequently after capturing an insect, perhaps to bring up some nectar with which to wash the insect down.

The return of spring brought many new flowers for Squeak to try, flowers that ordinarily bloom too early in the season for the hummingbirds here. Cut branches of forsythia, Korean rhododendron and flowering apricot were brought in for Squeak. He tried them all and, apparently, liked them all. Since he visited them repeatedly, I must assume that they contained nectar, even after being cut.

In the garden most hummers can be identified by the patient observer, not only by their looks, but by their eating habits as well. One of our female regulars, for instance, can easily be recognized by the soft yellow coloration where the male's gorget would be. She has been coming here for four years as an adult and her unusual throat, different from all the other females' throats, has never changed. She always takes a certain number of sips, always uses one of the Perky gravity feeders under the pine tree, and always sits on one particular bare branch.

Even though we also know her by her looks and other habits, another female who nests here can be identified solely by the way she uses the feeder. This female has been using our feeders for three years and in all that time still has not yet learned to save energy by sitting while eating.

One other female can always be told by the chirping she does in between sips, especially after the last sip. When she leaves the feeder, she spirals up and around the pine tree trunk, chirping incessantly.

Still one other female can be spotted by the way she feeds. She was born in 1987 and always uses the Perky bottle. However, she has never learned to use it the way the others do. She has never quite been able to master the art of sticking her bill through the front of the bee guard. She always ate from the side. As an adult she eats the same way. She was gone for a whole winter and never changed.

Many, perhaps all in their own way, have an

Approaching flowering quince—note the remains of an insect on his beak.

eating routine. I've noticed that many males have a "route." Certain birds will appear at the same place at precisely the same time each day. I could always expect a certain male to appear at the monarda each day at three specific times. Another male came each night just as it was getting dark to visit the coralbells (*Heuchera sanguinea*). One male was known sight unseen. The whirring of his feathers sounded exactly like a broadtail.

They really are such individuals, with their own particular habits. So was Squeak. He always took small sips and moved to alternate sides of his feeder between the sips, and he always stretched before going to the feeder. Squeak rarely tucked his feet in against his body while hovering in front of a flower or feeder. In typical young hummer fashion, he usually allowed his feet to hang quite freely. I was anxious to see what personal behavioral habits Squeak would be adopting once released.

Sleep

Everyone who has an avid interest in hummingbirds would welcome an opportunity to see one as it sleeps. I've heard accounts of people finding them asleep in bushes only five or six feet off the ground, but surely this is rare.

Because of their small size, hummingbirds have the greatest energy output of any warm-blooded animal and they lose body heat very rapidly—a far greater amount than larger birds do. In addition, they lack the down feathers that would enable them to increase their insulation by feather-fluffing. Hummingbirds must constantly replenish food in order to stay alive. Food in a hummingbird's crop will hold it over for only a couple of hours. Since they work on such a precarious energy balance and cannot always accomplish this over long periods, many become torpid, a sort of nightly hibernation, to conserve energy during periods of cold or when their reserves are not enough to sustain them. Torpidity, a state of reduced body temperature and metabolism, is the hummingbird's greatest safeguard against burning itself out. During torpidity a bird's temperature may drop almost to the temperature of the surrounding air.

Hummingbirds do not become torpid every night; incubating and brooding females as well as nestlings do not become torpid; and hummingbirds never enter torpidity when the temperature is over 95 degrees F. When a hummingbird is in such a state, it cannot fly. It may only be able to chirp weakly. If removed from its perch, it cannot regain its grip when replaced. Being in such a condition prevents a bird from being dislodged from its sleeping place during high winds. Torpidity is like a state of suspended animation.

Some birds, once torpid, emerge from their torpor before dawn, undoubtedly by some internal clock or mechanism. I believe that is the case with ruby-throated hummingbirds. Some do not become active again until warmed by the sun. Such is the case of the Chimborazo hillstar of Ecuador, an unusual hummingbird in many ways, a species dependent upon chuquiraga flowers and of which it is the sole pollinator. The Chimborazo hillstar lives just below the permanent snow line between 13,000 and 15,000 feet on the altiplano of the Andes and the slopes of the volcano Cotopaxi in one of the most severe climates in the world. Living and nesting at 15,000 feet, higher than almost any other bird, presents very special problems. On Cotopaxi, the air is thin and cold, ice crystals form every night, and snow and freezing temperatures are a frequent occurrence. The hillstar must torpidate to stay alive. During the night its body temperature may drop to as low as one-half of its normal temperature. As well as becoming torpid, this bird shelters in caves on the lava slopes of Cotopaxi to conserve additional energy over that which is saved in the torpid state. Not only is the temperature in the caves 1 or 2 degrees F. above freezing, but the problem of freezing to death as a result of radiation into the clear sky is eliminated.

Hummingbirds arrive in our garden very early in the morning. As a matter of fact, they arrive earlier in the mornings and leave later in the evenings than any of the other birds around except sometimes the cardinals. At the summer solstice birds begin arriving at 4:45 A.M.—always before the sun. At times early in the season and then again, late in the season, nights, and especially early morning hours, can be quite chilly. It is not uncommon for temperatures to dip into the very high thirties or low forties. Many of those birds had probably been torpid on those chilly nights. I am apt to conclude, therefore, that resumption of

Squeak slept on the skinny branch every night except one.

activity in the ruby-throated hummingbird occurs as a result of some internal rhythm and is not temperature- or sun-related. I do, on the other hand, remember certain young ruby-throats who spent all day, every day here, but didn't arrive in the mornings until the sun was shining in the yard. I only noticed that with two birds and I believe they were nestmates. It may be coincidence.

One of the decisions I had to make for Squeak was how much time to allow him for sleeping. That is, when to have the lights go on in the morning and when to have them shut off in the evening. Following a sunrise-to-sunset schedule here in the north where the nights are long would not be a good idea. In my opinion, the days would not be long enough for the bird to get the right amount of nourishment. I didn't want to keep summer hours either. I wanted to keep things as natural as possible under the circumstances. The closer to the equator one gets in winter, the longer the days are, so the days would, to some extent, be naturally longer than they are here. I decided, therefore, to have the lights turn on at 6:00 A.M. and go off at 8:00 P.M. This, I thought, would give Squeak ample daylight hours, actually more than he would have been getting naturally, and it would have also given long enough daylight hours to those plants affected by it with respect to flowering.

I was concerned about having all of the fluorescent lights turn off at the same time, so I had them turn off in two steps, the second half fifteen minutes after the first.

On his first night I left a light on outside the French door until he settled down. Twilight is gradual outside during the summer and I was afraid that he might be flying around and find himself suddenly and totally in the dark.

Of the several branches that I placed around for his benefit, he chose the skinniest one on which to sleep that very first night. He settled down facing the French door and slept at the very tip of that skinny branch. He went to sleep in *exactly* that same spot in *exactly* the same position each and every night thereafter except on March 1, when he decided to sleep on the branch at the north end of the room, his bird-watching branch. I could see him working himself up to that for three or four days when he was reluctant to leave that favorite branch toward the end of the evening. Once out of his system though, he returned to the regular routine that he had set for himself. While it is probably not set in stone, it may be very likely that hummingbirds retire to the same spot each evening to sleep. I have always been able to tell when it's the last drink of the day for the hummingbirds that regularly feed here—the final departure for the evening is always exactly the same pattern and direction from night to night and the flight is the same distance from the ground.

I don't know whether or not Squeak ever became torpid at night. I never touched him while he slept. It is doubtful, since his energy reserves were probably high enough that he didn't need to torpidate. Also, on several occasions, each well into the night, Squeak was observed stretching one of his wings. On one occasion I observed him scratching when he was supposed to be sound asleep. On another night he was pecking at his side—perhaps to dislodge a loose feather that had been itching or annoying him. Squeak was too active at night to have become torpid. One night I looked through the French door and, in the dim light cast by the outside porch light, could see a feather at the tip of his beak. I removed the feather, of course, but he had to have been scratching himself to dislodge that feather and have it land on his beak. However, he would puff up when getting ready to sleep. Puffing-up, or bristling the feathers, is what hummingbirds do to rapidly bring the body temperature down in preparation for torpidity by increasing the rate of dissipation of body heat. Since hummingbirds have no down feathers, puffing-up has the opposite effect of the feather-fluffing that other birds do. Perhaps there is just a slight lowering of body temperature. I can find no reference, however, to semitorpidity. An effort was made to approximate our average summer evening temperatures by maintaining a 58 to 60 degree F. range. During the daytime when sunlight filled the room, the temperature rose to about 70 or 75 degrees F. naturally. On raw or cloudy days I increased the temperature to 68 or 70 degrees F. The intention was to duplicate what I thought he would be getting in nature. Squeak had his own ideas. The hummingbirds that come to our garden are most active in the morning. Then they are next most active just prior to retiring for the evening. They feed frequently and are much more tolerant of one another at that time. Squeak was not active before retiring.

The end of the day came in three stages for Squeak. The first stage began at natural sunset. He was active all day long, flying around, visiting flowers and feeders, catching bugs, and preening. But, in spite of what I had planned, when sunset

71

arrived and the birds outside quieted down, so did Squeak. At that time, he would sit quietly at his choice spot of the time. Until February it was on a branch stuck in a mimulus plant under the fluorescents. He apparently liked the warmth there when the warmth from the sun was gone. He would leave the branch periodically, albeit infrequently, to visit a flower or a feeder and then eventually he would move about eight inches away to a different branch and hardly move at all. From late February on, Squeak barely sat under the fluorescents at all. Instead he began favoring the south end of the sunroom. He was especially fond of branches near the waterfall—either the one and only branch that he would use on the Island snapdragon plant or the branch stuck in the scarlet monkey flower (*Mimulus cardinalis*) plant. Nevertheless, wherever he sat at that point, he would hardly move at all. That was the second stage. Finally, about fifteen minutes before the lights would go off, he moved to the branch where he would be sleeping. That was the third stage and that's when I would pet him.

As time rolled on, and probably coincidental to the time spring migration might have otherwise begun, Squeak was less and less sedentary during the evenings. Time changed and habits changed with it. Evening activity increased tremendously over what it had been all winter. That little plant stake on which he had spent so many hours sitting fell by the wayside, never to be sat upon again. Of

The end of the day came in three stages for Squeak. Wherever he sat he would hardly move at all.

course, lengthening days is most likely the factor that precipitated these changes. By late January there was a noticeable difference in the time that he went to the skinny branch.

The most curious habit that Squeak had is what I call head-wagging. Each night after he settled down on that skinny branch, he spent from several seconds up to several minutes rapidly moving his head from side to side. I'm not sure what the significance of this action was. Perhaps it was instinctive, whereby the hummingbird assures itself that there are no enemies or even other hummingbirds around. I've seen other male ruby-throated hummingbirds perform this same movement. Not all of them, only certain ones—usually the most dominant male around, and I've only seen this behavior in the evening just before the particular bird would retreat to his sleeping place. I've always been under the impression that the bird was scanning its territory, searching for intruders. I suppose that Squeak considered the sunroom his territory and it may be, after all, that he was giving himself one final assurance that there were no enemies or intruders around before falling into that vulnerable state of sleep. If the lights were turned off while he was engaging in head wagging, he would stop instantly and close his eyes. Ordinarily, when he was tired and before drifting off to sleep, he would appear to have a little difficulty keeping his eyes open and he slept with them closed.

During evening inspections Squeak, on numerous occasions, was found to be retrieving some of the reserve from his crop as was evidenced by his swallowing or "gulping."

Tidbits

Once Squeak discovered that he could sit on a branch at the north end of the sunroom and watch the birds feeding outside, he spent a great deal of time each day doing just that. For the most part he just watched, occasionally pulling his head down and flattening his body when several birds would fly overhead. There were, however, certain birds to whom Squeak responded more than others. Foremost among them, and the first bird to which Squeak reacted, was a sharp-shinned hawk.

Hummingbirds are impudent and pugnacious little birds. It is comical to watch them chase birds many times their own size around the yard so fearlessly. They carry on in their devil-may-care manner regardless of what else is around and when all other birds are frozen during the presence of a

Expelling fecal matter, a hit-and-miss sort of affair.

hawk, hummingbirds just continue their comings and goings, fearlessly oblivious to any threat of danger. They apparently are confident in their ability to escape being caught. Jays will scream and holler, sending all the other birds scurrying for cover, but the hummingbirds just continue eating in their particularly defiant way. I had no reason to expect Squeak to behave any differently here, but he did. He would stop whatever he was doing and freeze when a hawk was around. He responded to the hollering of the blue jays by crouching and becoming absolutely still, as if he were out there too. Perhaps hawks are a problem to hummingbirds in their wintering grounds, although not such a problem over the summer range. He would stay in that frozen position until either I diverted his

Squeak had a cowlick, noticeable here as he visits apple blossoms.

attention or he heard some chirping outside.

Squeak also showed interest in the mocking-birds. Perhaps it was their flashy white patches. Every once in a while Squeak would see one scurrying across the garage roof and would attempt to chase it.

But, most of all, Squeak loved the cardinals. He would watch excitedly as the males chased one another, flying back and forth in front of and rushing right up to the windows, charging them. When he would hover in front of the windows watching the cardinals, the pitch or tone of his hovering would change. Perhaps his wings were rotating at a faster speed, for at those times he sounded like a drill.

Because Squeak showed a moderate amount of

interest in the birds outside, a mirror was set up in the sunroom for him. He seemed to dislike it, almost deliberately avoiding it.

Most hummingbirds are unable to walk or hop, depending on their wings for locomotion. When they want to move, even to change position on a perch, they put their wings into motion and, rising slightly above the perch, pivot around. They hardly ever land on the substratum. On April 27, I saw the closest thing to a hummingbird walking that I, or possibly anyone else, may ever see. Squeak landed on a shelf in pursuit of a fallen fuchsia flower. He landed about two inches from the flower and so was unable to reach it just right. He wanted to check the flower for nectar, but it was loose and each time he approached it with his beak, he actually pushed it farther away. As he continued to follow the flower, step by step, half-walking, half-sliding forward, he also continued to push it that much farther away. The movement was similar to the way a hummingbird sidles along laterally to move an inch or two on a twig, the same type of action except with a forward movement.

Hummingbirds are so small, and unless one is fine-tuned to them, they go unnoticed more often than not. People have stopped here and, while looking through the glass of the French door, have said, "How's the bird?" and not see him sitting on the skinny branch, no more than two feet directly in front of their eyes.

Expelling fecal matter is basically an involuntary action, a hit-and-miss sort of affair with no mind being given to it at all. This is not the case, however, when preparing to sleep. At that time, Squeak would lift his back end and shoot the droppings several feet away. Perhaps that was instinctive so as not to give away his location.

Hummingbirds can hardly be described without the liberal use of superlatives. Because most hummers don't sing, there is only one area in which they are ever said to be lacking, and that's voice. This is especially true with our North American hummers. In spite of this reputation, Squeak had quite a repertoire of vocalizations, from squeaky metallic clinks and soft, barely audible chirps to loud guttural chatter, and he barely did anything without at least a chirp. He would make that metallic clink noise after every sip of nectar, chirp while he was bathing, and respond in kind if I chirped to him. Voice does match size and, under ordinary circumstances, most of his adorable squeaky little chirps would go unnoticed.

All of the feathers across Squeak's back were sparkling emerald green and overlapping perfectly in a mosaic pattern. All, that is, except a few feathers dead center between the wings that crisscrossed one another and refused to lay flat. The effect of these crisscrossed feathers was especially noticeable by the air movement from his wings. While Squeak was hovering, the feathers lifted up and curved backward toward his head—Squeak had a pronounced cowlick! I have carefully examined all my photographs of other hummingbirds, as well as photographs of hummingbirds in books, and I have not seen even one other hummer with this unusual characteristic. Some day in the future, this cowlick, his trademark, may prove to be the clue to his identity.

3

Toward The Spring

The Molt

Molting is the gradual, periodic replacement of old and worn-out feathers. The molting season and the duration of the molt cycle is different in the various species of hummingbird. With some species the molt is an annual event, while others molt more than once each year. The process uses a great deal of energy and has a definite affect on metabolism. When feathers are missing, the body loses heat more rapidly than when the bird is fully feathered, thus requiring more fuel to keep the furnace going, and more power is needed when flying with missing wing or tail feathers. To compensate for this additional energy requirement, hummingbirds are often not as active during this period and some may even gain a little weight because of the inactivity.

Reference is scanty, perhaps even nonexistent, as to how often the ruby-throated hummingbird molts, and I've had to draw my own conclusion. Two, spring and fall, is a logical assumption based upon observation over the years. The spring molt precedes the breeding season and probably occurs, at least in part, prior to spring migration. At least some also molt in the fall prior to their departure for the wintering grounds. Every year we have several males in our garden that are in the process of molting. Gorgets, reportedly the last feathers to be replaced, are usually renewed toward the end of August. Birds are not sexually active in their wintering grounds and, furthermore, as migrants, they are subordinate to many other hummers. So I don't know why the gorget feathers are replaced except that they must just become worn. Young ruby-throats do not molt before leaving and we've only had one molting female here in the fall. This occurred three years in a row, including this past year, but each year it has been the same female. I don't know what the yellow-throated female does. Each year when she's finished nesting, she leaves and allows her young to have this territory for the remainder of the season. Most of the other females here do likewise. On the other hand, very many females have remained here right up to the end of the season with no signs of molting at all. Perhaps molting is sporadic, with individual birds having their own individual timetables as other birds do. For instance, you never see all the blue jays in the garden molting at the same exact time. Even among hummingbirds here, differences can be seen.

The molt is variously reported as beginning with the shedding of the first primary and finishing up with replacement of the gorget feathers, the hummingbirds' crowning glory and that which should be in the best condition for the breeding season. This is true at least as far as Anna's is concerned. The only hummingbird molting habit that has been studied in detail has been Anna's hummingbird, but there is no reason why one should not expect that the pattern would at least be similar. It has been reported that hummingbirds do not attempt to breed out of season because of the dormancy of their sex glands and it has been further suggested that until the new gorget is complete, the males don't even engage in display behavior.

Squeak's molt began in mid-January with the loss of a chest feather. On January 14, I noticed several pinfeathers on the chest and saw one chest feather fall out while he was scratching. Within a week he had pinfeathers on the throat, gorget area, breast, head, and his post-ocular spot, and was losing feathers every time he started scratching. As a matter of fact, he did an inordinate amount of scratching during that period. The loose

In early February new iridescent gorget feathers began to appear.

feathers must have either made him feel uncomfortable or itchy. Under ordinary and free circumstances, this would place the start of the molt prior to the spring migration.

Coincidentally, it was about that time that Squeak began what I perceived to be sexual behavior. It started small, with displaying in the shuttle-flight fashion, but once it started, it continued. I consider it sexual behavior because not only did he display, but he also mounted anything oval-shaped—a flower bud or even a small fuchsia leaf.

Within a few days from the time he arrived here, I noticed his one iridescent red spot, dead center at the lower part of the gorget area. It is not unusual for young male hummers to have one or more iridescent gorget feathers. Some have sev-

Squeak during his molt—notice the pinfeather sheaths on his head.

eral. I've seen them concentrated at the center of the gorget area, scattered here and there, and like a necklace across the border of the gorget and throat areas. One had such a bright band of iridescence there that I referred to him as "ring of bright feathers." The gorget is supposed to be the last area to molt, but Squeak's gorget started coming in even before he lost one primary. It began February 4 when a new iridescent red spot revealed itself. This was followed by additional iridescent gorget feathers and, before the end of February it looked as though his throat had been sprinkled with brilliant dust from rubies. The one red spot he had all winter always appeared to be very bright, but with the onset of new gorget feathers, the difference between the old and the new became very apparent and incomparable. Returning male humming-birds in the spring always look brighter than they do toward the end of the season. Apparently the feathers lose brilliance with the passage of time.

Squeak continued to lose and replace small body feathers at a rapid pace and by the end of February, I had picked up and saved lots of them.

This pace continued through March 4, when feather loss seemed to come to a standstill. For the next week, only one or two feathers were lost altogether. Then, on March 12, the molt resumed vigorously, even more rapidly than it had before. More feathers were found in the two-week period from March 4 through March 18 than had been found in the almost two-month period from January 14 through March 4. Feather loss wasn't as sporadic as it had been either. Squeak seemed to be primarily losing feathers from the same area, almost as if the line of feather loss was moving down the front of him from the bottom of the gorget area and working downward. With the two different levels of feathers causing him to appear sleek on top and puffy on bottom, he looked as though he were sitting snugly in a pecan shell, or maybe even the bottom half of an eggshell, or as if someone had just peeled away the feathers.

Around April I began to become quite con-cerned about the slow progression of Squeak's molt. He had been replacing contour feathers since mid-January and by April the smattering of iridescent gorget feathers had begun to coalesce, appearing to all who might capture a glimpse of his radiance that he had captured light, electrified it, and shot it back. However, he had not even started to replace the primaries and was still showing the juvenile tail spots. It should be noted that these feathers appeared to be in top condition. By early April ruby-throats are well on their way to being back on their breeding grounds and other males, I am sure, had long since completed their molts.

My concern was that perhaps Squeak was deficient in a particular hormone and perhaps that same hormone is responsible for fattening up for the fall departure. If that were true, Squeak's future might possibly be in jeopardy.

With this thought gnawing away at me, I placed telephone calls to two hummingbird authorities in an attempt to find out whether this might be a problem. It was indicated that, with the exception of Anna's, very little is known about molting in hummingbirds. However, this failure to have a complete molt, especially in juveniles, is not unheard of, and that it does happen. Perhaps production of the hormone that causes the molt is the result of excessive proteins consumed on the wintering grounds—food for thought. About a year ago, I had heard of a newly returning male ruby-throat that had only a small amount of iridescent gorget feathers instead of the full gorget. Since it was much too early in the season for it to be a

He looked as though he were sitting snugly in a pecan shell.

young hummer, I had been convinced that the person had been mistaken. Although I had never noticed it during all the years I've been watching hummingbirds, and while it may not be common, apparently it does occur and apparently she had been correct.

Whether or not Squeak would be breeding this year was doubtful, not so much because of the lack of any hormone, but because of the lack of a full and attractive gorget with which to attract a female.

One point that was made was that the males are not as strict about returning to their nesting grounds as the females are. Therefore, Squeak might very well just opt to remain here in our garden rather than return to the place of his birth—which

By April the smattering of iridescent gorget feathers had begun to coalesce.

may have even been as far away as Canada. It was also indicated that juveniles have only a general idea of where to migrate to in the fall, but are pretty much left on their own to make that first trip by their own devices. Imagine, barely a few months old and having to make such a journey. If a bird is successful, it will take the same route each year thereafter. So I should not be surprised if I were to find him at my doorstep next October expecting to winter here in the sunroom.

The possibilities that existed were encouraging and exciting. The chances would be good that he might make our garden his territory. Absent that, or perhaps in addition to that, he might make our sunroom his wintering grounds. What delightful prospects.

For the better part of April, molting was non-existent and I had resigned myself to the fact that I would not be saving any tail feathers (rectrices) or wing feathers (remiges) and I would not be seeing Squeak with a full, glow-from-within gorget. Then, on May 4, it started in again. I found twenty-six feathers on the floor under the branches where he sat to scratch or preen, including five or six from the head, where pinfeathers had again begun to appear, a couple of spotted feathers from the gorget area, and one of the secondaries.

I just could not help worrying about the way he was so slow at molting as well as fattening up for migration and hoping that the two weren't related.

Growing Up

In early January, Squeak began displaying, not in the large arc commonly associated with the ruby-throated hummingbird, but in that tight oscillation of only a couple of inches and up to a couple of feet commonly called the shuttle flight. I call it buzzing because of the noise that accompanies the display. In addition to any vocalizations, a mechanical noise is made during the display. I'm not sure exactly how that noise is produced, but it sounds as though the feathers are held at such an angle so as to cause air to pass over or through them, thereby creating a vibrating type of sound. Interestingly, the display noise sounds a great deal like the sound made when Squeak flew around the

Squeak began to mount buds after displaying to them—here it is a hibiscus bud.

His little feet moved forward and backward—front view.

Rear view.

During the display, Squeak, moving from side to side, fanned his tail each time he changed direction.

93

room drying his wings and, possibly, tail after his bath and shower. The first time he displayed, he displayed twice to the metal bars under the plant trays and once to the handle on one of the tripods. Perhaps small horizontal objects interested him.

By mid-January, just about when his molt started, Squeak expanded his display to include other objects such as a leaf or flower bud (also in the horizontal position). But, in addition to the displaying that he had been doing, Squeak began to mount the different buds after he displayed to them. And, although hummingbirds reportedly do not attempt to breed or engage in display behavior until their new gorgets have been completed, in my opinion Squeak was definitely showing sexual behavior. Apparently this behavior does not hold true for the ruby-throat, at least not this ruby-throat. Actually, the only real work that has been done, with respect to breeding out of captivity, has been as it relates to the Anna's, a hummingbird that breeds extremely early anyway. When Squeak would mount a bud, his little feet moved forward and backward, almost as if he were trying to stand on it, and at times even pressing into the bud as if he were trying to secure himself or hold it down. The time spent on any individual bud was never more than a few seconds after which he almost seemed to slide off.

This type of behavior—displaying and then mounting for a few seconds—continued for approximately one month. Then, around mid-February, he added a new dimension to this aspect of his personality. He began attacking the buds before he mounted them. First he would display to the unopened buds in his usual fashion and then, before mounting them, would stab at them viciously and repeatedly with his beak. This was always done as he passed from the right of the bud to the left. Consequently, there were many mangled phalaenopsis and fuchsia buds in the sunroom, each having numerous puncture marks on one side. Still, he only showed any interest in oval shaped objects in a horizontal position.

I'm not sure of what brought on each individual act of displaying but, seemingly spontaneous, it would begin with Squeak, head forward and lowered and neck sleek and outstretched, looking at something. He would then flick his tail. He appeared to get a slight muscle contraction at the base of the tail just before he would start the actual display behavior. He would then rush right up to the object of his affection and quickly begin his display, moving from side to side and fanning his tail each time he changed direction. He faced the object at all times, undoubtedly to exhibit the iridescent plumage of his gorget to its best advantage.

In addition to the dazzling aerial display flights to a female, a hummingbird may also engage in display flights as an aggressive gesture designed to show its territory, not only to members of its own

His gorget would be held in a concave position to concentrate its color.

species, but to non-hummingbirds as well. They are notoriously pugnacious during the breeding season. On a few occasions, Squeak even displayed to me. Once it wasn't just his usual shuttle display, it was an arc. A small one, but an arc nevertheless. First he sat on his branch just looking at me. Then, all of a sudden, the arc. Perhaps he was threatening me, in his own way telling me to get out, or maybe it was just a practice run.

By early March, Squeak added vocalizations to his repetoire of adult male hummingbird display behavior. The vocalizations sounded much like an extremely loud, sharp, high-pitched, and very rapid chatter and are in addition to the noise produced by the feathers when displaying. Occasionally after the above noted behavior, Squeak would perch on one of his branches and, with his beak slightly ajar, make a hoarse, squealing noise that sounded like air being slowly let out of something.

While Squeak was displaying, his gorget would be held, either voluntarily or involuntarily, I'm not sure, in a concave position, thus forcing it to face forward even more than it would otherwise, concentrating the color and making it much more attractive to a female or threatening to an adversary. This was especially noticeable when Squeak was viewed from the side. This action may also account for the gorget's extreme brilliance on certain occasions. We keep a clothesline up in the yard as a place for the hummingbirds to sit. If a male is sitting on the line and facing the house, the beautiful ruby-colored gorget is clearly visible. However, a difference in the gorget is detected immediately if another male arrives on the scene. The radiance then becomes so overpowering that the glow practically obliterates the rest of the bird from sight.

Making Friends

Each evening as Squeak perched on the skinny branch and before the lights went off, I would gently stroke his breast with one finger. He wasn't afraid and he either didn't seem to mind at all or was just tolerating it. Once, though, when I nudged him a bit, trying to get him to sit on my finger, he responded by flying over to the feeder. He was reluctant and I never pushed it.

The little female that stayed in the sunroom that snowy day in 1987 spent a considerable amount of that time sitting on my finger. At first she was somewhat cautious, but once she realized that it was somewhere to sit and that I wasn't hurting her, she was almost eager to take advantage of the perch. Later she appeared to be quite relaxed as she sat preening herself for stretches of up to ten or twelve minutes each. She did this repeatedly while she was here. She never approached my finger on her own but when I put my finger next to her and nudged, she sat willingly. Squeak, on the other hand, didn't exhibit any such signs of trust toward my hands for quite some time. Even when he finally did lose his fear of my hands, he was never willing to perch on a finger.

Right from the beginning, basically, I was able to get close to him. I was able to put my face as close to Squeak as the limit of my focusing ability would allow and it was always all right with him. He seemed to enjoy it when I would hum to him, often tilting his head and closing his eyes. At times he would just stare at me and he looked just like a bottle-nosed dolphin. He never minded my being close as long as I kept my hands away from him. If my hands were in my pockets or behind my back, everything was fine. That is, unless I was holding something that interested him. He had absolutely no qualms about being near my hands if they held something he wanted.

Hummingbirds are naturally inquisitive. Squeak was no less inquisitive here in this unnatural environment. After he had been here but a short while he became quite accustomed to my presence and grew very inquisitive about me. Within a couple of weeks he was deliberately touching me. He investigated everything, including my hair, my eyes, my cameras and tripods. He spent a great deal of time, several minutes at a clip, investigating my hair, especially at the back of my head. It may very well have been that he was merely looking for

At times he would just stare at me and he looked just like a bottle-nosed dolphin.

insects, or perhaps it was just curiosity, but he would go around behind me and investigate the hair at the back of my head. I suppose he thought that as long as he couldn't see my eyes, I didn't know that he was there. One day while investigating my eye, he stuck his tongue out and touched my lashes. He showed a remarkable amount of interest in my eyes, frequently hovering in front of them while his tongue darted in and out. Perhaps the pupil resembles the tube of a flower.

When I walked into his room wearing a floral-printed dress, he spent several minutes trying to figure out how to get nectar from the "flowers." Apparently he recognized them for what they are intended to be. I've seen him try to enter flowers that were pictures on catalog covers.

He was very interested when I talked softly to him and would cock his head, focusing in on me, and answer in barely audible chirps. Those endearing little chirps supposedly mean contentment and I like to think that they do. They are apparently age-linked, being common, for the most part, to juveniles, and I must admit that I heard them less and less often as Squeak grew up.

He was soon brave enough that he would follow me anytime I had something in my hand, floating along right beside me inspecting whatever it was that I was holding.

There were times, too, when Squeak would become angry. Primarily those times related to a change in his territory. One such time was when I moved a small-budded flowering maple that had grown too tall to fit under the fluorescents. He liked to visit that plant when he was at the stage where he sat under the lights. When he realized that it was gone, it almost seemed as if he were giving a "dirty look" to the fuchsia that had been put in its place, stretching his neck and pulling his head all the way back as if he were looking at something in sheer disbelief. He wanted that flowering maple put back where it had been and flew away and back over and over as if he expected the right one to appear upon one of his returns. Needless to say, I returned the plant to where it had been. I'm sure that he was satisfied as he immediately visited a flower and calmed down afterward.

Another time he was visibly angry when I hung a trailing kalanchoe plant slightly above and away from where he was to sleep. He liked the plant very much and visited it immediately and repeatedly when I brought it in, but didn't want it near his sleeping branch when he was ready to settle down for the night. He would get on the branch, look at the plant and immediately get off the branch again. He was waiting, I'm sure, for that new foreign object to disappear. Finally, I moved the plant for the night. I did that every night for over a week. By that time he was a little more amenable to it and I was able to leave it at that new spot permanently.

He would also become annoyed when I tried to clean his room. I'm sure he became angry. He would dive at me or fly straight at my face and then, at the very last moment, dip down to about chest level and up and over my head. After he would dive at me, he would go to a bare branch and sit with his mouth slightly opened, his threat posture, just looking at me.

When Squeak was very angry or frightened, his feathers were held tightly against his body and he appeared much thinner. So thin, in fact, that he appeared skinny in the neck area. On the other hand, when he was very relaxed, he would appear especially puffy. Ordinarily he was somewhere in between, slightly puffy.

I had wanted to form some sort of bond with

Squeak before I released him, not only to make sure that our garden would be his territory but to have a special relationship with him once he was on his own as well. I wanted our relationship of the winter to continue in a modified form during the spring and summer. Friendship would have to center around his needs and food, of course, would be the best bet.

I had tried several times during the winter to get Squeak interested in a small red tube that I had filled with a very sweet sugar and water solution, but I had been having poor luck with that approach. I also tried a small vial with a red ribbon tied around it, also to no avail. It wasn't that he wouldn't approach something that I was holding, because he would visit flowers as I held them up for him. I decided that I would have to offer the sugar-water solution in something more familiar to him, something like one of his feeders. That's exactly what I did. I used a Nektar-Plus feeder and made a 2-to-1 ratio solution of water and sugar and after eight or ten minutes of tempting, he tried it. He loved it and came back over and over again for more. He wouldn't leave me alone. Every time I walked into his room he would hover around me chirping and chirping, looking for a treat. I wanted the solution to be a special treat only and to serve as a bond. I didn't want him to be drinking it all the time, but he wanted it and he would poke all around me looking for it. Once, when I walked

Squeak and me.

into the room, he hovered around my face, chirping and getting closer and closer to my eyes, looking for his treat. He got so close to my eyes that I had to close them. The next thing I knew, he had inserted his beak into my nostril. He certainly made himself irresistible.

If I entered the room holding the feeder, he would spot it from across the room and would quickly and directly fly over to drink. He would then hover back and forth in front of it so rapidly and anxiously that I was barely able to turn the feeder around and switch it to my right hand. He would take one long drink and one sip. He would then fly over to the branch, sit for a few seconds, come back to the feeder, take one final short sip, and then fly to the other side of the room and sit.

He was finished. He would chirp after each sip and everytime he sat. Of course, after every feeding, his bill was scraped, first one side and then the other, across a twig.

Unlike most birds that beat their wings, hummingbirds rotate their relatively long wings at the shoulder with little flexing at the wrist or elbow and receive power on both the up and down strokes. During hovering the wings move horizontally in a figure-eight pattern and cycle about eighty times per second. The air movement created by his hovering wings was so strong that when I fed him about level with my neck, it felt as though there were a fan right next to my feet. Not only is the down draft strong, but the air movement would even set plants swaying several feet away laterally.

If I entered the room without the feeder, he would actually follow me around, chirping, until I left to get the feeder. It was quite difficult for me to resist when he begged for the sugar-water. I wanted the solution to be particularly sweet, especially later when I, hopefully, would be feeding him outdoors, but I knew that the 2-to-1 ratio was much too sweet, so I began to gradually increase the solution of water and sugar to 3-to-1.

Until that time, a turning point, Squeak appeared to be oblivious to the door, seemingly unconcerned about what was on the other side. All of a sudden he began watching for me on the other side and upon seeing me, would fly right up to the door, hovering all around and looking for his treat. It's unbelievable how quickly he learned and it only took one taste of that sugar-water. All of a sudden he began sitting on that skinny branch at all different times. After all, it's a perfect place to sit for a good view of approaching nectar. When he saw me approaching the door, he would drop down to the door handle and hover there waiting for me to come into the room. He quickly made the association of either the sight or sound of the handle turning with the receipt of his treat. It was noticeable that he was especially active about bug-catching once he started having that solution. Perhaps it is instinctive for him to keep his diet balanced. At any rate, I believe it certainly was best that I had to leave him most of the day while I went to work. This kept him using the balanced Nektar-Plus for the major part of the day.

The only time that he would not take the offered solution was the time I walked into his room wearing a T-shirt with a picture of two broad-billed hummingbirds and a castilleja plant. He fanned his tail, hovering from side to side, and then flew over to a branch on the other side of the room. It was apparent that he didn't like what he saw on that shirt. I changed the shirt and when I went back into the room he was back to his usual behavior. That wasn't the first article of clothing at which he had shown disapproval. He wasn't very fond of the sweat shirt with the picture of a cat with large eyes on it either.

Squeak was especially active about bug-catching toward the end of the day, just as the other hummingbirds appear to be in the garden, and there were certain places where he hunted more than others. One of those places, of course, was the waterfall, a natural magnet for little gnats and aphids. Squeak would also rush into certain plants to stir up the whiteflies, with the scarlet monkey flower plant always yielding generous numbers for him to catch.

The weather had warmed up nicely and by mid-April I decided to move the mimulus plant outside to the lath house. Actually, I was happy to get rid of some of the whiteflies. Squeak, however, missed the plant almost immediately. When he would rush in the way he did to stir them up, his efforts were unproductive. Failing to find any insects in a place where they had been available before, Squeak moved to the branch at the north window and tried the same action toward some of the other plants.

In an attempt to help him out, I disturbed some whiteflies from the undersides of a particular fuchsia. To my surprise, Squeak flew over immediately to where my hand was and started catching and eating one whitefly after another in a feeding-frenzy manner. He showed absolutely no uneasiness about being so close to my hand whatsoever and took complete advantage of my help for as long as I was willing to give it. After helping him only two or three times, Squeak learned that all he had to do if he wanted my assistance was to go to that fuchsia plant, hover and chirp to get my attention. All during fall and winter Squeak had taken care of his own protein needs with no interference from me and had done very well for himself at that. But, as winter turned to spring, building a bond between us became more and more important to me and becoming involved in what he liked was the way to do it. In no time at all, Squeak and I became an effective hunting team.

He always knew what he wanted and always knew exactly how to get it. He begged and pestered me for sugary treats by hovering around my head, chirping and dancing back and forth in front of my eyes or hovering all around my hands (of all places) looking for the feeder. Sometimes he would chirp softly while circling my head and then hovering back and forth in front of and so close to my eyes that I could no longer focus in on him. He would watch for me through the door and greet me the minute I entered the room. The very last thing I did each night before Squeak went to sleep was to bring the feeder of sugar-water in to him and hold it while he sat on the skinny branch lazily sipping one last time. When he was ready for his shower and bath, he would wait for me to enter the room, fly over to the bathing area and, while sitting on the branch under the fluorescents,

Squeak having a sugary treat.

chirp and look at the cattleya leaf, waiting for my compliance. And, when he wanted some hunting help, he managed to get that across to me as well. He'd sit on the branch, look at the fuchsia where we hunted the whiteflies, look at me, look at the fuchsia again, and chirp. Or he would go to that fuchsia and hover over it, doing nothing else, waiting for me to come over and do my part. I was supposed to know what he wanted and I did. I've always thought that a vacuum cleaner would be an effective way to control whiteflies but Squeak worked without electricity. I think he rather liked having me around and would hover around my head just looking at me for no apparent reason. No matter what I may have been doing, Squeak would dart over to investigate. Eventually it got to the point that anything that I held in my hand was regarded as a possible food source and was promptly investigated. And, if he wasn't hovering around my face or flying as closely as possible to me, he'd fly over to wherever I was and sit near me. He liked sitting right behind me best; of all the branches in the sunroom on which he could sit, he always chose the one closest to me.

Once the turning point had been reached, Squeak became more responsive to me than he had ever been and even though I like to think otherwise, I'm sure that he consented to be my friend because he, like most other animals, is such a little opportunist. Nevertheless, by late April I felt that we had really and finally become friends and my only hope was that it might carry over to the outdoors.

The Release

Spring rolled around far too quickly in 1989. It seems as though it was just yesterday that I discovered Squeak in the garden. He had been my ray of sunshine for the whole winter, but I knew all along that eventually I would have to start thinking about releasing him and I knew that it would be difficult. Never before in my life had I wished it were still January when May rolled around, but this year has proven to have been different.

As the inevitable drew near, it became increasingly difficult for me to accept, and not nearly as clear that releasing him was the best and right thing to do. Of course my rationale had become biased by my innermost desires. I envisioned many different scenarios, all of which had Squeak wanting to stay. I wanted to keep him here, protected from the sometimes harsh world of nature, and it wasn't as though he had been chomping at the bit to get out. He had accepted his entire stay here very matter-of-factly, but this is not where he belongs. All I had to do was look at him and it brought a smile to my face and my heart. I'd watch him do all the little things he did and as I watched, I'd beam. How was I ever going to be able to do it? He had been doing the same things here all winter that he would have been doing outdoors: visiting flowers, hunting for insects, bathing, preening, loafing, and sleeping. He had never known the hardship of fighting elements to arrive at some foreign destination, of being chased away from a flower that some other hummingbird had claimed for its own.

It is so hard to let go of something you've

treasured as much as I'd treasured Squeak, even when you know it's the right thing to do. This would turn out to be one of the toughest decisions that I had ever had to make and stick with. Whether or not to release him was thought out very carefully and with very mixed emotions. All the pros and cons were weighed diligently. If Squeak were to stay in, a regular source of food, plenty of flowers and insects would always be available to him, longevity would virtually be assured, and sleeping in the rain (and as much as they like rain, I'm sure they don't like it when it's cold and constant), pesticides, spiders' webs, and other such perils would be unknown to him. But, if he were to be released, he would have interaction with other hummingbirds. The longer he stayed here, the further removed from nature he might become. It could become ten to twelve years of living in one room and that would not be fair.

I don't know where this bird had come from originally—it may have been twenty, thirty or fifty miles away—nor did I know whether or not he would be going back. My greatest fear was that when I opened the door he would just take off and I'd never see him again, and I knew if that were to happen, it would break my heart.

Initially the plan was to release Squeak during the first week in May, hopefully a day or two before any other hummers returned. Being the first one here might give Squeak an edge on becoming yard boss. I wanted him to make our garden his territory so his progress could be monitored. It had been suggested to me by more than one person that I have someone band Squeak. As with everything else, banding has its pros and cons. After consideration of all the factors, I decided against it as being unnecessary, possibly undesirable, and of no benefit to Squeak, only to a person who might find him.

The first week in May, however, was unusually cold and rainy, certainly too cold, I thought, to expose Squeak to the elements. It was decided to postpone his release for several days. On May 10 it was pouring and I couldn't help wondering where Squeak would have been sleeping had he been released. I began to reevaluate my decision. Perhaps I should scrap the release plan altogether.

But then, after the first week of May when other hummers began to return, everything changed, and my thoughts changed too. Although he had not been chomping at the bit to get out, it was quite another story when he spotted other hummers outside. He became very excited, chattering and flying rapidly back and forth. Or he would hover in front of the window, watching them. Somehow they always knew he was there also. I walked in one day to see Squeak and another male hovering beak to beak with the window in between them. I knew what had to be done. May 14 would be the day that he would be released. The weather was back to normal and, besides, it was Mother's Day.

The morning of the release went about as usual, eating, preening, a bath and shower, preening, begging for treats, preening, hanging around loafing and begging for treats. About 10:30 A.M., I finally got up the nerve to make a move. I opened the back door for the first time since last fall and stood there with his treat in my hand. He came over periodically for a sip and each time I stood farther outside. Three times he came out, took a sip, and flew back inside. The fourth time I stood a couple of feet out of the door. After almost one-half hour of coaxing, he finally came all the way out. After a drink he flew over and inspected the buds on a fuchsia hanging under the porch's overhang, along with the windows and the lattice-work of the overhang. He then lifted up and over the roof of the porch toward the front of the house and that was it. That was the last I saw of him.

I must admit, tears welled up in my eyes and for an instant, just a split second, I was sorry for what I had done. Not so much sorry that I let him go, just sorry that he didn't stay. Words simply cannot express the heartache that I felt when he failed to come right back. Maybe hummingbirds are just free spirits that don't form any attachments. They do lack the typical avian social structure.

He's a free bird now. Although it was not what I had been expecting, I had hoped that he would hang around, eagerly accepting our human hand-outs. As hard as it might be, I knew that I'd have to be willing to say good-bye.

I look for him everywhere, even now. I keep the screen off one window in the sunroom hoping that one day he'll fly in to beg for his sugary treat or shower, or that one night he'll decide that he wants to sleep on the skinny branch. I've even replaced one of the regular feeders with a Nektar-Plus feeder; it should make an excellent training feeder for new hummers but, mainly, I want Squeak to find a familiar sight should he decide to return. I know I'd feel much better if he'd make that one appearance that would tell me that he's making out just fine on his own. It rained his first night away.

It seems like only yesterday that I worried so about whether he would make it through the winter all right. Now, in retrospect, it all seems so easy and natural. I suppose that being rescued and making it unscathed through a winter that would have otherwise brought about his demise is happy ending enough for me.

As far as looks are concerned, right now I'd recognize him. When he gets a full gorget, he will no longer look the same. When I do see him, if he acts the way "old Squeak" acted, I shall surely recognize him. Until then, every time I see a male

Parting shot—the last photo taken of Squeak, May 14, 1989.

sitting around looking in the direction of the house, I'll take an extra good look—and each time I'll hope.

The pleasure of his company was fleeting, as are so many of the best things in life. I often think about what I was told that I might expect. Perhaps the sunroom will be his imprinted wintering grounds. Perhaps when the fall arrives, we will again have a winter guest, a living jewel among the flowers.